Day of Reckoning

A play

Pam Valentine

Samuel French — London
New York - Toronto - Hollywood

CHARACTERS

Ethel Swift, country woman, middle-aged
Angela Brownlee, an infant school teacher, 20s
Mavis Partridge, 83
Sally Martin, Army wife, early 40s
Gloria Pitt, Honorary Secretary, middle-aged
Pauline Morris, Geoffrey's wife, 50s
Marjorie Organ, a breezy, outspoken woman, 30s
Geoffrey Morris, a vicar, 50s

The action of the play takes place in a village in rural England, or Scotland, or Wales

Time: the present

SYNOPSIS OF SCENES

ACT I

House lights dim. Sound of voices rising from chatter to crescendo. Firm rapping of a gavel

Pauline Ladies! Ladies, please!

The voices subside

...Thank you. Now, it's been a long—and I hope—fruitful evening. But we're all tired, tempers are getting a little frayed and I think we should get our diaries out, and fix a date for—what is it we're fixing a date for, Hon. Sec.?
Gloria Item fifty-three, Madam Chairperson. Fix date for first meeting of Summer Fête Committee. Sometime in January.
Pauline Thank you, Hon. Sec. Right then, ladies. A night in January that suits us all.

There is an immediate crescendo of voices giving nights when they cannot attend: "Thursdays no good", "I can't do Wednesdays", "Mondays are out", "It's patchwork on Fridays", "Tuesday's car maintenance", etc.

Sound of the gavel

Ladies! Ladies! Surely we can all find one night in January...

The CURTAINS *open*

SCENE 1

The village hall. The present

A hall of the old type. Drooping curtains at the rear conceal a platform. Cumbersome radiator is R. The door L leads to the toilets and the kitchen. The door R leads to the car park. There is a window L with more drooping floral curtains. There is a notice board with many pieces of paper tacked up; trestle tables folded against a wall; a stack of chairs; here and there are remnants of Christmas: a drooping paper chain, a touch of tinsel, a sprig of dead holly

Ethel Swift enters R. *She is a country woman of middle years, keeper of the*
village shop and fount of all local knowledge

She switches on a light, looks round, shivers. She goes to the radiator, feels
it and makes a noise of disgust. Goes to the trestle tables and drags one DL.
She attempts to erect it. Sings a doleful carol

Ethel   In the bleak mid-winter, frosty winds made moan. (*She tugs to*
                  release a table leg)
                  Earth lay hard as iron, snow lay like a—bugger! (*She has*
                  caught her finger. She puts it in her mouth)

We hear a motor bike revving outside. Puzzled, Ethel looks towards the
door R. *The bike pulls away. The door* R *opens*

  Angela Brownlee enters, hesitantly. This is her first committee meeting.
  She is an infant teacher in her twenties. Plain, shy, and longing to be loved

Angela Hallo, Mrs Swift! It's just started to… Oh! What have you done?
Ethel Caught me finger in this dratted table, Miss Brownlee, that's what I've
  done!
Angela Oh, poor you! I bet it … you know… (*She makes an expression of*
  pain)
Ethel I shouldn't be surprised if the Youth Club hadn't been at them legs.
  Very funny they'd think that was.
Angela Oh, surely not…
Ethel They super glued the seat in the churchyard last summer. That one the
  old folk sit on to look down at the traffic on the bypass. We had to call the
  ambulance out to old Daddy Ludlow. Stuck fast, he was.

Angela is taking her coat off

  I should keep that on if I were you. Them radiators is barely luke.
Angela I'm quite hot actually.
Ethel You do look a bit flushed. (*Casually*) Do you know I thought I heard
  a motorbike outside. Just before you came in…
Angela Oh! That was Raymond. Raymond Treadwell. He gave me a lift.
Ethel (*shocked*) Raymond Treadwell gave you a lift?
Angela He passed me as I was coming up Cherry Pie Hill. So he stopped and
  … he had a spare helmet.
Ethel I'm sure he did. Look, Miss Brownlee, no offence, but you've not lived
  here long enough to know—it do not do to socialize with a Treadwell.
  Specially you being an infant teacher an' all.

Angela But he stopped and... I didn't want to be ... you know ... rude.
Ethel I'm not saying be rude! I'm saying have nothing to do with him. And what's he doing with a bike? He's only sixteen.
Angela Eighteen, actually.
Ethel Which makes it worse. (*Having succeeded with the table, she now puts chairs round*) Course, the trouble is you haven't made any friends in the village, have you?
Angela Not really. It's my fault. I'm so ... shy with people.
Ethel Not with the kiddies, you're not. I've seen 'em in the playground. Crawling all over you, they are.
Angela Oh, I'm all right with children. It's grown ups. I know what I want to say—in my head I hear myself saying it. Then I try to say it and I can't. That's why I've come on the Committee. To see if it'll help me to ... you know...
Ethel Well. If you want to say something tonight you say it. I know it's your first time and we all know each other and you're a stranger and you'll feel awkward when you speak but you say it.
Angela I'll try. People don't seem to see me...
Ethel Stick your hand up, then!
Angela Stick my hand up?
Ethel Yes. Like this. (*She gives a forceful salute*) See? Up! Right up!

Mavis Partridge enters R. *She is eighty-three, deaf when it suits her, a law unto herself and doesn't miss a trick. She has a large bag with knitting inside. She looks at Ethel's raised arm and copies her*

Mavis Heil Hitler. Cold i'n't it? I reckon me corsets have froze to me bum.
Ethel You should never have come out, Mavis, not on a night like this. Not with your chest.
Mavis Pardon?
Ethel Oh. We're having a deaf night.
Mavis I saw your lips move——
Ethel —But you didn't hear what I said.
Mavis But I didn't hear what you said. Think I'll go and spend a penny. 'Fore all the others get here. I never like going in front of the Vicar.
Ethel If he comes.
Mavis (*passing Angela*) Hallo, my duck. I didn't see you there.
Ethel This is Miss Brownlee, Mavis. She's the——
Mavis I'm not stopping long. There's snooker at eleven.

Mavis exits L *to the toilets*

Angela Snooker?

Ethel You ought to see her watching American Football. She gets that worked up she throws herself out of her chair.

Angela How old is she?

Ethel Eighty-three. Eighty-four the day of the fête.

Angela Has she lived here long?

Ethel Always. And her family before her. You can't move in the churchyard without falling over a Partridge.

There is a persistent knocking on the door R

Angela I'll go!

Ethel Hang about! Hang about! It might be the Youth Club on the rampage. (*She goes to the door*) Who is it?

Sally (*off; calling*) It's I! Sally Martin. Do please open up. My arms are breaking.

Ethel opens the door

Sally Martin enters. An Army wife in her early forties. Immaculately casual. Confident and slightly condescending to other ranks. She carries a large object concealed in a blanket

Thank you, Mrs Swift. It's really beginning to come down out there, you know. (*She mock staggers to the table and deposits the object*) This would be a night when Colin's on manoeuvrers. I've had such a struggle. And after the most exhausting day. My cleaning lady went AWOL. Which made me late for my quilting class. Mad dash home, then off to my stint at the Oxfam Shop, then straight from there to that ghastly supermarket where four—four, mark you—checkouts were on the blink. Who'd be me? Oh! Hallo, Miss Brownlee, I didn't see you!

Ethel You've met, have you?

Angela opens her mouth but Sally beats her to it

Sally Oh yes, we're old chums. I pop in to the school and help with the slow readers…

She sees Ethel is tugging at the blanket tied round the large object

Oh! Mrs Swift! Do be careful!

Ethel (*hurt and huffy*) Only trying to help.

Sally (*redoing the blanket*) It's a rather lovely stone cherub. I bought him when we were stationed in Akrotiri.

Ethel Why ever have you brought him along tonight?
Sally Because one of those stupid oafs who are building our conservatory knocked the end off his arrow and I can't bear to look at him. Mrs Moxon can have him for the bric-à-brac stall.
Ethel Mrs Moxon's not coming tonight. And she's not doing the bric-à-brac neither.
Sally What?
Ethel She's starting B and B in May. Or so she says. I've told her folks nowadays expects en sweaty bathrooms but she won't have it.
Sally *Quelle disastre!* I wonder who we can possibly get to take her place...

Angela tentatively raises an arm and continues to jerk it up and down as Sally speaks

There's Cynthia Brinscombe ... she might do it ... unless they do get that Hong Kong posting ... she'd be marvellous ... none of this "Oh well, give me ten p then" nonsense... (*She becomes aware of Angela's arm*) Are you all right, dear?
Angela No. Yes. It's just if ... you know ... you can't find——

The door R is thrown open. Gloria Pitt enters. She is a doctors' receptionist and Honorary Secretary to the fête committee, of middle to late years. Seemingly competent but actually clinging on by a thin thread. She brushes snow from her shoulders and looks towards Ethel

Gloria Would you mind, Ethel?
Ethel (*darting forward*) Wheel it in, Gloria.

Gloria takes a newspaper from within her coat and hands it to Ethel who spreads the pages on the floor

Gloria exits and re-enters, wheeling a sit-up-and-beg bicycle. A basket strapped to the front contains an ancient and bulging briefcase

As Gloria speaks, she first removes and polishes her glasses, then divests herself of her anorak, scarf and woolly hat

Gloria What a night... Oh, hallo, Mrs Martin—I've had such a rush. I thought Surgery would never end. Everyone wanted to see Dr Summers. Nary a one could I persuade into young Dr O'Connor. And he's such a sweetie. Then the usual rush home to settle Mother, do her tray, leave everything to hand, then just as I was leaving, she said Sooty had gone missing, so it was hunt the cat for twenty minutes. And I went out of my way to drop some pills into Mrs Partridge and she wasn't in. Oh! Hallo, Miss Brownlee! I didn't see you.

Ethel Mavis is here, Gloria. Been here ages.

Gloria (*looking round*) Where?

Angela Gosh! She went to the... Do you suppose she's all right?

Ethel Oh, yes, she'll be... (*She is struck by a sudden thought*) Why don't you pop and have a look? Only sometimes she nods off.

Sally In the loo?

Ethel She's eighty-three, Mrs Martin. She nods off wherever she's comfy. (*To Angela*) Go on, dear, run and see.

Angela (*thrilled*) Oh! Right.

Angela exits L

Ethel watches her go then turns to the others

Ethel If you hear one word of gossip about that girl you're to knock it on the head.

Sally Gossip? What gossip? She couldn't say boo to a goose!

Ethel Then it's a pity she didn't say boo to Raymond Treadwell.

Gloria Oh dear.

Sally Which one of the Treadwells is he?

Ethel The one Vicar caught whipping the candles off the main altar.

Gloria It was during a power cut...

Ethel You'd see good in anyone, Gloria, you would.

Sally But—she's so timid, and shy, and ... plain.

Ethel Exactly, Mrs Martin, ripe for the plucking.

Gloria Probably nothing but silly rumour. You know what this village is like. Do you remember when——

Ethel Thank goodness it was dark...

Sally When?

Ethel Mm? Oh, when she got on his bike...

They all turn to Ethel, eager for more, Pauline Morris enters R. *Wife to the Reverend Geoffrey Morris and chairperson of the fête committee. In her fifties. She carries a capacious bag and has an air of distraction. As she speaks, she takes various items from the bag*

Pauline Hallo, everyone, sorry I'm late. We've got the grandchildren staying and I had to cook two suppers. Now they're watching something highly unsuitable on the box that they swear they're allowed to watch at home and quite honestly I was too tired to argue. They're up at the crack of dawn and permanently ravenous. It's all too much for poor Geoffrey, he spends most of the day locked in the study.

Ethel Locked in there now, is he?

Pauline (*instantly worried*) Isn't he here? He left a good ten minutes before me. Said he wanted some thinking time.

Ethel Oh well, I shouldn't worry. He's probably ... thinking.

Mavis and Angela enter L

Mavis And there weren't no proper roads in those days. Sea of mud it used to be most of the year. Mind you, it was safe to walk out at night, mud or no mud. Not like now. All this rape everywhere you look. You live alone, do you then?

Angela (*nervously*) Yes...

Mavis I hope you've got strong locks. Mind you, if they want to get in, they'll get in...

Gloria I called round to you with some pills, Mrs Partridge. How's the chest?

Mavis Pardon?

Gloria (*loudly*) How's the chest?

Mavis Nicely ta. I've not brought nothing up for at least a week. When are we starting? Cos I'm going once we've sorted out the bran tub. (*She sits next to the radiator*)

Pauline Is the bran tub far down on the agenda, Hon. Sec.?

Gloria Hang on... (*She tips a file on to the table, scattering papers. She takes one and searches down it*) Bran tub ... bran tub...

Pauline (*to Angela*) What a cold night for your first meeting. Are you full of bright ideas?

Angela opens her mouth to reply but Sally cuts in

Sally Pauline, do look! I'm giving this little chap to the bric-à-brac. (*She unties the blanket wrapped round the cherub*)

Gloria Here we are. Bran Tub. Item thirteen. It comes under...

The blanket falls. The cherub's back view is revealed. The ladies are looking at the front. The little chap is obviously male

...small attractions. (*She looks up and sees the cherub*)

Sally It's a Spanndic.

Ethel A what dick?

Sally Spanndic. A Danish sculptor of some repute. (*To the cherub*) You've lost your arrow, haven't you, pet?

Mavis He's got plenty of everything else.

Ethel Don't be coarse, Mavis.

Sally I was hoping Mrs Moxon could put him in her garage. Now he's chipped I can't bear to look at him. But if she's not doing it, I don't know what to——

Ethel We can put him in the back of my shop. If he gets lonely, he can talk to the bacon. That's Danish.

Pauline (*looking in her bag*) Do you know, in the rush of getting here I've forgotten the biscuits.

Ethel Oh, we can do without biscuits.

Mavis A cup of tea's not a cup of tea without a biscuit to dip in it.

Pauline It isn't, is it? I'll just pop back. Shan't be two ticks.

Ethel No need for that. We can pop this … thing, to my shop and I'll pick up some biscuits. I'm closer'n what you are.

Pauline That's sweet of you, but I think I will just scoot back. It'll give me the chance to check on the children.

Ethel But——

Pauline I might bump into Geoffrey.

Pauline exits R

Ethel Fall over him more like. (*She looks in the bag Pauline has left on the table. She holds up two packets of biscuits*) Forgot the biscuits … ginger nuts and garibaldis! (*She puts them back*)

Mavis No custard creams?

Ethel He'll be in the *Coach and Horses*.

Gloria I thought he was off it at the moment.

Sally He certainly wasn't "off it" at the Brinscombes on Friday. He was well and truly plastered. Cynthia was very good about it. If he'd broken my Caithness vase I'd have spat blood.

Ethel One of these days it'll get back to the Bishop.

Gloria He still conducts the services quite properly.

Ethel Does he? Daddy Ludlow's funeral? Did anyone know of any just impediment? (*To Angela*) I expect you've heard about Vicar's little problem?

Angela No, I——

Ethel Ah. Then best we say nothing. If an alcoholic chooses to remain anonymous, that's his prerogative.

Gloria I wouldn't call him an alcoholic.

Ethel I would. Why he took up with vicaring I'll never know. (*To Angela*) He came to it late.

Sally It's Pauline I feel sorry for. I mean, you marry an up-and-coming executive and ten years later he announces he's going to be a priest. Her social world must have turned completely upside down. She showed me photographs once of their old house. Beautiful. With a garden that swept down to the river.

Ethel Handy for chucking the bottles in. (*She goes to the cherub*) Let's get this thing round to my shop while we've got the chance.
Sally Good idea. (*She wraps the blanket round the cherub*) You know, if Colin said he was leaving the army and going into the church, I think I'd divorce him.
Ethel (*helping to pick up the cherub*) If my Charlie got any kind of job, I'd die a happy woman. Come on. Let's go.
Mavis Bring us back some custard creams.

Between them, they carry the cupid to the door. Angela springs to open it

Sally and Ethel exit chatting

Mavis—seemingly in her own world—knits away at a large blanket of many coloured wools. Gloria and Angela smile at each other awkwardly

Gloria Such a chilly night!
Angela Yes.
Gloria Even chillier than last night, wouldn't you say?
Angela Yes.
Gloria Yes.

Gloria springs into action, making Angela jump

Agendas. (*She puts agendas round the table, straightens them pedantically. She looks at Angela*)

They smile again

Did you have a good Christmas? Lots of fun times with your family?
Angela I don't have a family. My parents are dead.
Gloria Oh dear!
Angela I went to my aunt. In Huddersfield.
Gloria Oh, well that was——
Angela My uncle died in November. It was her first Christmas … you know … alone.
Mavis I bet that was jolly.
Gloria Good that you have … someone.
Angela Yes.

There is a pause

Gloria Pencils.

Angela jumps

People never bring them.

Gloria takes pencils from her bag and places one by each agenda

So... How long have you been living here now?
Angela Five months.
Gloria Really?
Angela Yes.
Gloria Not very long, then?
Angela No.
Gloria And are you ... settling in?
Angela Mm. Yes. Sort of.
Gloria Good. And have you ... made any friends?
Angela Not really. Oh, people have been very ... you know ... but...
Gloria But you're not rushing into anything. Very wise. It's so easy when one is lonely to act a little ... impetuously. Two things one should never hurry—choosing a puppy and making new friends. That's one of Mother's.
Angela Does she live with you?
Gloria Yes. Well, me with her really. It's her cottage.
Mavis It'll come to you when she goes.
Gloria Oh, I hope that's a long way off, Mrs Partridge. (*To Angela*) We're such—chums, you see. My goodness, I would have done some foolish things if I hadn't had Mother keeping a weather eye.
Angela Really?
Gloria Goodness yes. (*She straightens the agendas*) The biggest joke of all was when I wanted to go to Africa. And work in a mission hospital.
Angela Africa! Gosh!
Gloria "You in the jungle?" Mother said, "You get prickly heat just sitting by a light bulb." Actually I don't. She was exaggerating.
Angela How old is she? Your mother?
Gloria (*still in Africa*) What? Oh! Eighty-seven.
Mavis And I'm eighty-three.
Angela I know. And you're a wonderful knitter, aren't you?
Mavis It's a blanket. For the Third World. I don't have to pay the postage.
Gloria It just shows that one should be very careful.
Angela Sorry?
Gloria Before rushing into ... anything.
Angela Oh. Yes.
Gloria And you know, my dear, in a small community, people are so quick to ... talk.
Angela (*quite bewildered*) Yes...

The door R *opens. Marjorie Organ enters. A horsy woman in her thirties.*
Bright, breezy and outspoken. She brushes snow from her shoulders

Marjorie Sorry I'm late. All the way to bloody Newbury to pick up a bloody chestnut—cost an arm and a leg—and what do I find? The minute I get the beast back? It's a windsucker! No vices! I'll give the bloody woman no vices. (*She sees Angela*) Oh, a stranger in our midst.
Gloria This is Miss Brownlee, Marjorie. She's the new infant teacher.
Marjorie Is she indeed! Miss Brownlee. That's a bit of a mouthful.
Angela I'm Angela, actually.
Marjorie (*extending a hand*) Hallo, Angela Actually. I'm Marjorie. Mugsy to my friends.

They shake hands

Mavis Here, the next time your horse does its doings outside my hedge, chuck it over. It'll fall right on my rhubarb!
Marjorie Come off it, Mavis. I may call a spade a spade but I don't ride round with a bloody shovel! I'll send Jack round with a load. All right?
Mavis Nicely ta.
Angela What's a ... you know ... windsucker?
Marjorie Ah! Someone who asks intelligent questions. Well...

Marjorie begins to explain to Angela as Ethel and Sally enter R

Ethel Evening, Marjorie. (*To Gloria*) Is he here?
Gloria I'm afraid not.
Sally Oh really... I've masses to do at home. We've people to drinks tomorrow, I could make a start on the canapés...
Marjorie In other words instead of... (*She snorts air out*)
Ethel He'll be no use when he does get here.
Gloria Oh, Ethel!
Ethel Well, he won't.
Marjorie You get... (*She sucks air in*)
Gloria He could have popped in to old Mr Williams. He's very near the end.
Marjorie Then—to top it all—he starts weaving. This is weaving. (*She sucks, snorts, and weaves*) All sixteen two of him. And I'm trying to lug him out of the box.
Angela Gosh!
Mavis What's the chance of a cup of tea? I put the urn on when I went to the lavvy.
Ethel If you have a cup now and another cup later, you know what'll happen. You'll be backwards and forwards all night.

Mavis I can't help that I wanna cup of tea.
Angela I'll get you one. Excuse me, Marjorie. (*She goes towards the kitchen*)
Marjorie Mugsy!
Mavis Two teabags and three sugars.
Angela Right.

Angela exits L

Marjorie Sweet child.
Ethel Let's hope she stays that way.
Marjorie What do you mean?
Gloria Ethel, least said…
Ethel If she keeps off the back of his bike there won't be no more to be said.
Marjorie Whose bike?
Ethel Raymond Treadwell's, but it's not to go beyond these four walls.
Gloria I think I'll ask her round one evening. For a game of Scrabble. Mother's in bed by seven, we can have something on a tray.
Sally She won't come. I've asked her to drinks twice now.
Mavis She's coming to me on Saturday. We're gonna have faggots and peas and watch Gladiators. (*She leans forward, almost tipping over*)
Ethel What are you doing?
Mavis Me wool's wadged under the radiator.
Marjorie I'll get it. (*She kneels down, gets the wool and blows on it*) Yukkie poo. It's covered in dust.
Mavis That don't matter. Mrs Willis says it's all sand in the Third World. Wouldn't suit me.
Marjorie There's some old muck under here. It needs a bloody good sweep. Toffee papers, fag ends, bus tickets… (*She pulls rubbish out and spots something*) Jumping Jehosophat! That's very nice, I must say!
Sally What is it?
Mavis (*looking*) Oh, I get a lot of them chucked in my hedge.
Marjorie It's a frenchie.
Sally (*looking*) How perfectly horrid.
Ethel (*looking*) Well, if that doesn't beat all. You can bet your life one of the youth club put that there.
Gloria Not necessarily.
Ethel Oh Gloria, wake up. It won't have been the Horticultural.

Angela enters with the tea. She sees them looking at something on the floor

Angela What's the matter?
Marjorie Someone's chucked a rubber johnnie under the radiator.
Angela A what?

Marjorie A rubber johnnie! A french letter! A condom! I don't know any other words for it...
Angela (*looking*) Gosh ... is that what they look like...
Marjorie If they haven't been used. Obviously had a refusal. Whoever he was.
Ethel Raymond Treadwell or I'm a Dutchman. You know he came in my shop and asked if I sold them!
Sally Better that than unwanted babies.
Ethel Better they don't do it at all. Mucky little devils.
Mavis Willie warmer.
Marjorie What?
Mavis You said you didn't know another word for it. Willie warmer.
Marjorie Oh, Mavis, that isn't a willie warmer. You knit willie warmers.
Mavis Oh no, I don't.
Ethel I'm glad the Vicar *isn't* here. I wouldn't know where to put meself.
Sally The thing is—what are we going to do about it?
Marjorie Well, we can sweep it up. Or we can kick it back! (*She looks at them*) Motion carried?
Gloria Carried unanimously.
Marjorie Right. (*She kicks the rubbish back*) Now can we please make a start. It's half past now.
Mavis (*holding out a hand to Angela*) Ta!
Angela Oh! Sorry.

Angela gives Mavis the tea. Mavis pours it in the saucer and slurps

Gloria Unfortunately, Marjorie, we have no Madam Chairperson.
Ethel She's gone looking for the Vicar.

Mavis slurps again

  Mavis! Must you?
Marjorie He isn't on the toot again, is he?
Sally It rather looks like it!
Marjorie Oh Christmas!
Mavis (*blowing on the tea*) He's searching for his God.
Ethel Well, he won't find him in the *Coach and Horses*. Oh, come on, Gloria. Make a start.
Gloria Is that the wish of all of you? That I open the meeting?
Ethel Yes!
Gloria Then let's be seated.

They select their chairs

Marjorie (*to Angela*) We'll sit here, shall we? (*She picks up an agenda*) Holy Joe! It's even longer than last year's.

Gloria Right then, ladies. In the absence of—are you stopping over there, Mrs Partridge?

Mavis Pardon?

Ethel Come and sit here, Mavis. Or we shall only have to shout.

Mavis No, you won't. I can hear you.

Gloria Very well. In the absence of Madam Chairperson I shall have to wear two hats, so wearing my— (*she mimes putting on a hat*) Madam Chairperson's hat, I declare the meeting open and now— (*she mimes taking one hat off and putting another one on*) wearing my Hon. Sec.'s hat——

Mavis We don't usually start with a game, do we?

Gloria Item one——

Pauline enters R. *She smiles across reassuringly*

Pauline So sorry. All well. Just a case of crossed wires. (*She turns back to the open door*)

The ladies exchange sceptical looks, then fix their gaze on the door

Do come in, Geoffrey! We want to close the door. (*To the ladies*) It's really settling out there now.

Geoffrey Morris enters. He is in his fifties. A forbidding man, who does not tolerate fools, he is capable of moments of great charm. Although not drunk, he has had sufficient alcohol to make him very aware of his own co-ordination and slightly truculent

Pauline brushes snow from his shoulders. He makes a noise of irritation and looks at the ladies

Geoffrey I think my wife is confusing me with one of the grandchildren.

They laugh politely. He removes his coat

Apparantly there was some confusion as to the time of the meeting.

Ethel goes to speak

Gloria (*swiftly*) Yes. I'm sorry about that.

Geoffrey hangs his coat on a non-existent hook. The coat falls to the ground

Pauline What are you doing, Geoffrey?
Geoffrey It's perfectly obvious what I'm doing. Hanging my coat up. But someone has seen fit to remove the hook.
Ethel (*to the ladies*) Hook? What hook?
Gloria I'll get one put up—put back, Vicar.
Geoffrey Thank you.
Pauline Let's sit down. (*She puts a hand under his elbow*)

He shakes it off and walks very deliberately to the table. He is about to sit when, remembering the hook, he feels behind him to make sure there is a chair. He sits. Pauline sits

Now has everyone been introduced to everyone? Marjorie? Have you been introduced to Miss Brownlee?
Marjorie (*with a warm smile to Angela*) Oh yes! We're old chums.
Geoffrey Miss Who?
Ethel Brownlee, Vicar. The new infant teacher.

Angela raises a tentative hand. Geoffrey looks at her

Angela (*mortified with shyness*) Me. That's me. We have met. At the school. Hallo!
Geoffrey What?
Ethel She said hallo, Vicar.
Geoffrey Oh.
Gloria Now, if we all have our agendas…

Geoffrey looks at the table in front of him. Pauline points to his agenda

Geoffrey What?
Pauline Your agenda.

Gloria from his other side pushes his pencil towards him

Gloria And your pencil.
Geoffrey How kind. Agenda. (*He lifts it up then puts it down*) Pencil. (*He lifts it up then puts it down*)
Pauline Have you formally opened the meeting, Hon. Sec.?
Geoffrey Agenda. Pencil. Finger paints. Plasticine.
Gloria As good as, Madam Chairperson. We were just going to——
Geoffrey Is that coffee you're drinking, Mrs Partridge?
Mavis Tea, Vicar.
Geoffrey Tea.

Pauline Then I think we should crack on with——
Mavis Tea. The cup that cheers…
Ethel But not inebriates.

*Geoffrey looks at Ethel, is about to speak. Pauline shakes her head at him.
He rises. Sways. Knocks his chair over*

  Geoffrey exits L *to the kitchen*

There is an anguished silence

Pauline He's … very tired.

The ladies make soothing noises

  I'll just go and see if—do carry on. (*She goes to the door* L) I am so sorry.

  Pauline exits L

Ethel picks up the chair. There is a pause

Gloria Apologies received…

SCENE 2

Much later that night

All coats have been removed. Teacups abound. Agendas are scattered

*Gloria has a pile of notes. Mavis's knitting has lengthened alarmingly.
Geoffrey has gone from tipsy to tetchy. Marjorie sits astride a chair*

Marjorie Look! See what I mean? If the child had sat upright like this—as
    instructed—instead of fidgeting and farting all over the place, he wouldn't
    have fallen off!
Sally You do all know that it's ten forty-five?
Marjorie Nice straight back. Trot trot. No prob.
Pauline But he did fall off?
Marjorie He bit the horse! Of course he bloody fell off!
Ethel What about more helpers?
Marjorie What about them? Every year I ask and every year it ends up me
    and Jack. Doing the lot.

Angela raises a hesitant hand

Sally Could we possibly move on?
Gloria We've been half an hour on these pony rides, Madam Chairperson.
Geoffrey Oh, much longer than that, surely!
Marjorie More helpers…

Ethel puts a hand under Angela's elbow and shoves her arm sky high

Ethel I think Miss Brownlee wishes to make a point, Madam Chairperson!
Geoffrey Miss Who?
Pauline Brownlee. (*She smiles at Angela*) The chair recognizes Miss Brownlee.

Everyone looks at Angela. She struggles to speak

Geoffrey Is she all right?
Ethel It's her first time, Vicar.
Marjorie Spit it out, lovey!
Angela I was going to say—wanted to say—about the ponies—I mean, I'd love to do—help to do—bric-à-brac—but … but if not—and I don't mind—I could help Mr and Mrs Organ with the pony rides!

Looks are exchanged. Angela feels she has said the wrong thing

Marjorie There is no Mr Organ, lovey.
Angela Oh. Sorry. Well, you and your friend Jack. If he doesn't mind.

All heads turn to Marjorie

Marjorie Let's clear the fences, shall we? Jack is a she, not a he. And Jack is my dear friend and business partner.

There is a pause

Sally (*offering a plate*) Garibaldi, anyone?
Mavis Takes all sorts…
Pauline Could you minute that, Hon. Sec.?
Gloria Minute what?
Pauline More helpers for the pony rides.
Gloria I already have. Item forty-seven. Insurance.
Pauline Ah! Now we know that——
Geoffrey Why do we have to waste time talking about insurance? We simply

pay it, don't we? With the usual outrageous increase because a weather vane blew down in a freak storm over Orpington.

Gloria Normally yes, Vicar.

Geoffrey Normally yes, Vicar. What does that mean? Normally yes?

Ethel This'll be Colonel Godfrey's poodle.

Sally My husband has asked me to say that he——

Geoffrey Forgive my ignorance, but what has a poodle got to do with our insurance?

Ethel It slipped its collar, didn't it, Vicar?

Geoffrey Did it?

Ethel During the Best Behaved Bitch Class. And three of the police demonstration alsatians chased it into the Craft Tent.

Pauline Did we ever settle up with the glass blower, Hon. Sec.?

Gloria Yes. But it was pricey.

Marjorie Fancy entering the bloody thing while it was on heat.

Mavis Have they still got that dog?

Ethel No, Mavis. They had it put down.

Mavis I expect that's what they'll do to me. I shan't mind. I don't never want to be a burden. Is there any more tea in the pot?

Angela I'll go and see.

Angela takes Mavis's cup and exits L

Geoffrey But what has a poodle got to do with——

Ethel And they went straight out and got another one.

Sally I see no point at all in domestic animals. Mud, mess, and no thanks.

Gloria Can we come to a decision on this, Madam Chairperson?

Geoffrey Or on anything?

Pauline Our treasurer was going to investigate different insurers. So perhaps you could have a word with him?

Geoffrey What do you mean "Have a word with him"? Why isn't he here?

Sally looks at him with hostility

Pauline Our Treasurer is Major Martin, Geoffrey.

Gloria Who did say when he took the job on, Madam Chairperson, that he would be unable to attend many meetings.

Geoffrey Did he? Then why take the job on?

Sally He took the job on, Madam Chairperson, because he was given to understand that no-one else was willing or able to give it the considerable amount of time it demands. But I'm sure he would be more than happy to stand down.

Pauline Oh, Sally, please no. It's so difficult to—find the right person.

Geoffrey What do you mean? Any fool can add up a row of figures.

Sally Really? Then I suggest you find another fool. Excuse me. I think I need a breath of air.

Sally picks up her handbag and exits R

Gloria Oh, dear...
Pauline Geoffrey——
Geoffrey A word in the kitchen?
Pauline Would be a good idea...

Pauline exits, passing Angela who enters with a cup of tea. Geoffrey follows

Angela tiptoes to Mavis

Mavis Ta. Weren't there no ginger nuts?

Angela is in torment at the thought of re-entering the kitchen

Angela Er...
Ethel Oh Mavis, don't be so demanding!
Mavis Sorry, I'm sure. I shan't speak again.
Marjorie How long's all this going to take?
Gloria Poor woman...
Marjorie Which?
Gloria Both really. But it's unlike Mrs Martin to be so ... sensitive.
Ethel I wouldn't defend him if he was my husband. And I'd seen what she saw.
Marjorie Who? Saw what?
Ethel Her! Mrs Martin. Last Tuesday.
Gloria Ethel, it's probably just gossip whatever it is.
Ethel Gossip is what you hear. Facts is what you see. With your own eyes. Through a window. And better you hear it from me, Gloria, than from someone who wants to make mischief.

Pause

Last Tuesday it was. I was delivering a box of groceries—I knew she was out because she'd just been in and he's never there in the daytime, so when I saw a strange car in the drive I thought best have a look round, I thought. So I did. And there they was.

Pause

Marjorie Who? Who was?
Ethel Him. Major Martin. And this woman. He was on the settee and she was
stretched across him.
Angela Gosh!
Gloria Perhaps she was a relative?
Ethel Oh, wake up, Gloria.
Mavis What are you talking about?
Ethel What I told you yesterday. In confidence.
Mavis Oh that. Have we done the bran tub yet?
Ethel Yes, dear, we have. (*To Angela*) She's getting muddly. Go and admire
her knitting.
Angela I already have.
Ethel Do it again, there's a kind soul. It brings her back to the real world.

Angela crosses to Mavis

So anyway—laid across his lap she was, drawers round her ankles, skirt
round her ears.
Marjorie What was he doing?
Ethel Chastising her. With a hairbrush. Bristle side down.
Marjorie Bloody man needs gelding!
Ethel I couldn't stop because I had frozen food to deliver—and anyway, who
wants to watch filth—and as I drove off she drove up.
Marjorie Who? I'm completely lost here!
Ethel Mrs Martin! So she must have gone in and caught them while they was
at it. I mean—imagine the shock! Your own husband and a trollop. And
she's not long had that settee because when the delivery man came, he
couldn't find the——

Gloria nudges Ethel as Sally enters, composed

But as I say, it's probably nothing… (*To Sally*) Feeling better, dear?
Sally Yes, thank you. I apologise for the dramatic exit but I could feel myself
losing control. However. I've done some deep breathing. And all is well.
Mavis It never did us any harm, did it, Ethel?
Ethel What didn't?
Mavis A good spanking.
Ethel Mavis——
Mavis She says you're not allowed to chastise the children no more. And I
said it never did us any harm. (*To Angela*) You can keep that crochet hook.
Angela Thank you. (*Thrilled, she joins the others*)
Ethel Don't lose it, cos she'll want it back.

Pauline and Geoffrey enter. She is tight-lipped but smiling brightly

They sit. She looks at him expectantly

Geoffrey Er … it seems that I have—once again—blotted my copy book. Or—to quote my dear wife—"Gone too far this time". Which is, of course quite true. I am an irritable old fool and I must—as they say on school reports—"Do better". (*He smiles at Sally with the engaging air of a penitent schoolboy*)

Sally looks at him without expression. Everyone waits

That isn't quite as we rehearsed it, but I am most truly sorry, my dear. Most truly sorry.
Sally (*with charm*) Apology accepted.
Geoffrey And most charmingly, thank you.
Ethel Ah! Wasn't that lovely?
Pauline Hon. Sec.?
Gloria Yes?
Pauline Next item?
Gloria Oh! Right. Bear with me… (*She shuffles through papers*) Er… Item forty-eight. The tea tent. (*She looks meaningfully at Pauline*)
Pauline Ah, yes…
Ethel What about the tea tent?
Pauline We—we were wondering if you're happy to continue with the running of it?
Ethel Meaning?
Pauline Meaning exactly that. It's an arduous task, a mammoth load to carry, year after year, and if you feel you would like to … have a rest, you only have to say. You mustn't feel that just because you've been doing it for twenty-three years we expect you to always do it.
Ethel All right. What's this all about? Who's stuck their two penn'orth in and complained?
Mavis You won't get better sandwiches than what Ethel makes. Egg and cress, ham and tomato…
Ethel This is that Mrs Brinscombe, isn't it? She wants to take over, doesn't she? Been in the village two minutes, stuck a lamp post in the garden and a fiver in the church plate and thinks she owns the place.
Mavis Salmon and cucumber, cheese and pickle…
Sally Cynthia doesn't want to do it, actually.
Mavis Fairy cakes, rock cakes…
Ethel Oh. It's been discussed then?
Mavis Jam tarts, shortbread…
Marjorie You did say last year that you'd had enough.
Ethel What I said was I'd had enough of being set next to the bowling for a pig. That's what I said!

Pauline So what then? Are you happy to carry on?
Ethel Yes.
Pauline Good. Thank you.
Gloria Do you wish that minuting, Madam Chairperson?
Pauline Yes, Hon. Sec. And would you— —
Ethel But I want re-siting.
Pauline Re-siting?
Ethel Re-siting.
Pauline Where to?
Geoffrey Does it matter?
Ethel Yes, it most certainly does matter, Vicar.
Gloria Madam Chairperson, shall I minute that Mrs Swift wants re-siting and put it in on the agenda for our next meeting?
Mavis And you was too close to the toilet tent.
Sally I loathe that word.
Marjorie I don't know what's wrong with lavatory. (*To Angela*) What do you call it?
Angela The children say some funny things. Tinkle house. Poo poo room.
Geoffrey Are we going to talk bogs all night?
Pauline Mrs Swift—I cannot see why being close to the … convenience tent—should affect you? After all, people can have their refreshments and then wash their hands.
Ethel Flies.
Geoffrey Flies?
Ethel Flies. The toilet tent brings them in.
Sally Actually that is a valid point. Chemical lavatories are quite disgusting. A horrid smell and yes, there are flies.
Mavis It was worse in the old days. We had a two seater. And come Friday nights when mother gave us our jollop— —
Geoffrey We are going to talk bogs all night…
Gloria We do still have another seven items to attend to, Madam Chairperson.
Geoffrey Dear God…
Ethel I know what'll happen. I'll get minuted and I won't get moved.
Geoffrey Oh, move her! Move her!
Gloria It won't be easy, Madam Chairperson.

General conversation begins. Pauline bangs her gavel. They jump

Pauline Is it your wish that Mrs Swift be moved?
Marjorie OK with you, Angela?
Angela Oh… Yes.
Marjorie OK with us.
Sally Anything to hurry things along.
Pauline Mrs Partridge?

Mavis What?

Pauline Have you any objection to the tea tent being moved?

Mavis It was my idea in the first place…

Pauline I shall take that as yes. Very well, Mrs Swift——

Ethel Thank you.

Pauline Next item, please.

Gloria (*slowly going mad*) One moment, please, Madam Chairperson. (*She writes*) All assented… Thank you. Item forty——

Ethel I'll swop with the craft tent. That'll do nicely.

Sally Oh, I'm sorry but that isn't possible. The heat in that marquee is unbearable now and if we're moved to a non-shady spot——

Gloria I knew this would happen.

Geoffrey Then why didn't you say?

Marjorie Why can't the tea tent swop with the brass band?

Geoffrey Must we have a brass band? Thump, thump, thump…

Ethel Or I could go where the pony rides are. It's flat and it's shady.

Geoffrey One breath of wind and selections from *Showboat* are flying round the field…

Marjorie If you try shifting me you can whistle for your pony rides.

Pauline Could we try to be constructive in our comments? There really is little point in people——

Mavis I've locked.

Geoffrey She's what?

Ethel Locked. Hang on, Mavis. Hang on.

Ethel goes to Mavis and helps her stand. She moves her arms up and down

Mavis Go easy!

Pauline She's getting worse, isn't she…? (*To Gloria*) Should you perhaps have a word with the doctor?

Gloria (*rifling through her notes with mounting tension*) What? Oh … yes … probably…

Pauline (*softly*) Eighty-three … arthritic … bronchitic…

Sally Can we get on?

Geoffrey Can we go home? (*He starts doodling*)

Pauline It is very late. Perhaps we could adjourn and——

Gloria I'm sorry but we cannot adjourn in the middle of an item. For one thing, it wouldn't be proper. And for another, I'm the one who has to make sense of all this at the end of the day.

Ethel returns

Ethel Are we packing it in?

Pauline Our Hon. Sec. would like us to complete the business in hand first.

Ethel Oh. What business it that?
Gloria (*very crossly*) Re-siting your tea tent!

They look at her

I'm sorry but I do come here at the end of a working day. (*She flutters through papers*)
Marjorie Sorry, Ethel. But you're not having my spot.
Ethel Fair enough. No tea tent. And I would point out that all ingredients are supplied at cost.
Pauline Oh dear...
Geoffrey Suggestion?

They look at him

It may be far too simple a solution, but if you shift the bowling for a pig, the tea tent can stay as is and ditto the craft tent and the pony rides. Which would seem to solve the problem.
Ethel And where do we put the toilet tent?
Geoffrey It's amazing, isn't it? Even as we speak, world leaders are solving international problems. Men of science are splitting atoms. Medical experts are curing the incurable. And we—we happy few—cannot find somewhere to put a toilet tent.
Ethel Course what we really need is bigger venue...
Sally I see little point in stating the obvious.
Ethel I know you're under strain, dear, but don't be snappy.
Sally I beg your pardon?
Gloria Oh!

They look at her

I've just found a note that I did intend to mention earlier—Councillor Williamson.
Pauline What about him?
Gloria If we want him to open the fête, could we let him know because he's getting very booked up.
Sally Who by? Frightful little man.
Mavis Bruce Forsyth'd be a draw.
Ethel Excuse me—we've left my tea tent, have we?
Gloria Oh! And another note—Mr Moody must know how many floats we want by the end of February.
Mavis Shirley Bassey ... she's another...

Angela raises an arm

Pauline Miss Brownlee?

Angela Well, I've looked at this plan—of where all the stalls go and if we swap the bowling for a pig with the first aid tent and put the tinkle—toilet—convenience tent behind the first aid tent everyone can stay where they are! (*She collapses in exhaustion at the effort of speaking out*)

Marjorie Well done!

Ethel You can't.

Geoffrey (*ominously*) Why not?

Ethel Because the first aid tent has to be near the main gates in case we ever have to call an ambulance. It must have immediate access.

Geoffrey It's probably completely irrelevant, but have we ever had to call an ambulance?

Pauline No. Never.

Ethel What if a woman goes into premature labour? Or a man has a heart attack? Or a child chokes on its own vomit?

Geoffrey Bags I the heart attack.

Gloria Do I minute all of that? Or part of that? Or none of that?

Mavis Excuse me all. I'm going to pay a little visit. (*She rises and hobbles across*)

Ethel Do you want a hand, Mavis?

Mavis (*pausing*) No, thank you. I may be eighty-three, arthritic and bronchitic, but I can still find me way to the lavvy.

Mavis exits L *with dignity and an air of martyrdom*

Ethel And that's with a dead battery in her hearing aid.

Sally Look, I'm sorry, but I really must go.

Pauline Actually, Sally, I think we've all had enough for one night.

Geoffrey rises

But just before we do go——

With a sigh, Geoffrey sits

I wonder, Hon. Sec., if you'd mind quickly running through tonight's main points.

Gloria Main points?

Pauline It might save confusion next time, we've covered so much...

Gloria Main points. Right. I am in some chaos here and it might take me a moment to sort my papers out because it is rather unsettling to to stop before the full agenda is completed but—— (*Rising, she clears space in both directions*)

Papers fly around. Some land on the floor

Ethel Whatever are you doing, Gloria?
Gloria I am making space. To assimilate my notes.
Geoffrey It's all on her pad, isn't it?
Gloria No, Vicar, it is not "all on her pad". Some of it is "on her pad" and
  most of it is on separate sheets which I number and take home so that when
  you receive the minutes of tonight's aborted meeting, it will make sense.
  To you and to me.
Marjorie (*to Angela*) Storm warnings!

Gloria attempts to collate her notes

Geoffrey Oh, really. Why do you silly women——
Sally (*to Geoffrey*) I beg your pardon?
Pauline Don't bother, Hon. Sec., you're very tired and——
Gloria (*ignoring her*) Page one ... page two...
Sally (*to Geoffrey*) "Silly women" is a most offensive phrase.
Geoffrey All I meant was——
Gloria Page five. Where's page five?
Pauline I shouldn't have asked. It doesn't matter.
Angela Is it under the table? (*She dives beneath the table and emerges with
  a paper*). Page five. And there's more down there. (*Again she dives below*)
Marjorie I'll help. (*She joins Angela under the table*)
Sally "Silly women". It's like ... being called "love" by those illiterate louts
  building my conservatory.
Gloria Page six——
Ethel Gloria, do leave it be.
Sally (*to herself*) Huge great sweaty bodies. Taking mugs of tea with their
  great hard hands...
Gloria I have a very demanding job, you know. Blood samples, urine
  samples, faeces samples. Piled up in my In Tray.
Pauline Mrs Swift, she isn't well!
Ethel Gloria...
Sally (*to herself*) And they never ask to use my cloakroom. They must go
  somewhere ... zips half undone ... buttocks showing...
Gloria And Mother. Always Mother. Eternally Mother. Her breakfast tray.
  Her lunch tray. Her supper tray. Her Horlicks tray.
Sally (*to herself*) In my garden. That's where they go. Fouling my specimen
  shrubs.
Gloria And her pills. Her breakfast pills. Her lunch pills. Her tea pills. Her
  supper pills.

Mavis enters

Mavis Oh! I'm out of pills!

Ethel Not now, Mavis. Come on, Gloria my duck. You come along of me. I'm going to take you home. Give you a brandy. And tuck you up with a hot water bottle.

Geoffrey Heaven…

Gloria No-one knows … no-one has any idea… Do you know what my life is? My life is a tray.

Ethel There now! Sh, sh…

Mavis She needs a good tonic. (*Mavis returns to her chair*)

Ethel takes the sobbing Gloria to the door and dresses her in her outdoor gear. Pauline follows with her coat over her arm and helps to dress Gloria. Marjorie and Angela are under the table collecting papers. Sally takes a compact from her bag and powders her nose. Geoffrey watches her. Marjorie looks out from under the table

Marjorie All clear!

Marjorie and Angela emerge from under the table. Marjorie puts all the papers into Gloria's bag

And, believe it or not—this was a quiet night. (*She takes the bag to Ethel*)

Angela Gosh! (*She picks up her coat*)

Marjorie returns and holds it for her

Thank you.

Marjorie Pleasure.

Ethel Will someone see that Mavis gets home all right?

Pauline Not to worry. I'll take care of her.

Ethel Oh! And there's Gloria's bike.

Pauline Leave it to me. And thank you, Mrs Swift, thank you so much!

Ethel Let's tuck your scarf in, Gloria. That's right. Off we go.

Gloria My notes…

Ethel Just don't worry!

Ethel and Gloria exit

Pauline (*going to Mavis*) My word, Mrs Partridge! You've done some knitting tonight.

Mavis Well, I've asked and asked what size beds they have in this Third World. No-one knows, so I knit 'em all king size.

Pauline Sally, could you pop Gloria's bike in your Land Rover and dump it at her back door?

Sally Of course.

Pauline Geoffrey, if you help Sally with the bike, she can drop you off after. Ready, Mrs Partridge?

Mavis I expect so… 'cept I had a crochet hook when I come and now it's gone and disappeared. (*To Marjorie*) Don't forget my dib dobs!

Mavis follows Pauline and exits R

Marjorie I won't! (*To Angela*) Want a lift? It'll be fetlock deep out there.

Angela Gosh, thanks. That's … you know … very kind.

Marjorie Oh, I'm an amazingly kind person. You'll find out as you get to know me better. *En avant*, then. Night, all.

Marjorie and Angela exit R

Sally is applying lipstick, aware that Geoffrey is watching her

Geoffrey My dear, that "silly women" remark, it was just one of those silly phrases that we silly men sometimes use. But once again if I have offended——

Sally You are most truly sorry.

Geoffrey Yes.

Sally (*rising and getting her coat*) And do you truly mean that?

Geoffrey (*holding her coat as she puts it on*) Being truthful is one of my many problems.

Sally turns, looks at him and pauses for a moment

Sally I suppose we had better deal with "the bike"!

Geoffrey Yes.

She takes his face in her hands and kisses him

Thank you. (*He pauses*) You must know that my life is in absolute turmoil.

Sally As is mine.

They look at each other then kiss again

CURTAIN

ACT II

Scene 1

The village hall. The day of the fête, a hot July day. The last hour before the opening

A trestle table is erected. Cardboard boxes stacked against the wall. Plastic bags abound. General chaos

There are sounds of banging and shouting off

Geoffrey, dressed as Friar Tuck with a padded stomach, is trying to open the window

He is banging at it as Pauline enters, R. *She is dressed as Maid Marian. She has several bulging carrier bags*

Pauline It's locked. (*She puts the carrier bags on the table and starts sorting through old clothes*)
Geoffrey Locked? Locked?
Pauline Locked.
Geoffrey Where's the key?
Pauline I have no idea. (*She holds up a pair of trousers*)
Geoffrey (*looking at them*) Those are my gardening trousers.
Pauline Were. I gave them to the Good As New who have rejected them as not good enough.
Geoffrey The key, Pauline. Where is the key?
Pauline I've no idea. Probably Miss Pitt knows. But under the circumstances I don't suppose we'll be seeing her.
Geoffrey The hottest day of the year. A building with a corrugated roof. And a window that no-one has had the foresight to unlock. I think I'll smash the glass.
Pauline Do. (*She continues to look through the clothes*)

Geoffrey sees a pair of binoculars on top of another bag and examines them

From Major Godfrey.

Geoffrey (*looking through them*) They're rather good...
Pauline He suggested thirty pounds.
Geoffrey Did he? (*He puts them on the table*)
Pauline I'm going back out. You'll have to stay here.

He looks at her

We can't leave the hall unattended. There are silver cups behind that curtain.
Geoffrey And for how long am I to be marooned in this sauna?
Pauline Until someone comes who can stay until the next person comes and so on.
Geoffrey And so on and so on and so on...
Pauline Oh, if Mrs Partridge comes in——
Geoffrey Wish her happy birthday. You are possibly the fiftieth person to remind me.
Pauline Then don't forget. We'll cut her cake later. After we've cashed up. Another reason for someone to be here. Money will be coming in all afternoon. Have you got your walkie talkie?
Geoffrey (*taking a phone from a deep pocket*) Yes, Herr Commandant.
Pauline You can keep an eye on things from the window. (*She goes to the window*) You can see as far as the swings.
Geoffrey Oh good. What a joyful time I shall have.

Pauline goes to the door

Pauline The Bishop rang again.
Geoffrey Ah...
Pauline He's very anxious to speak to you.
Geoffrey Obviously.
Pauline He's phoned three times.
Geoffrey Then he is indeed an anxious little Bishop.

Pauline exits R

Geoffrey goes to the window and looks out. He takes his phone and speaks into it

Hallo? Hallo? Hallo? Base to Warden Nine. Hallo? (*With an impatient noise he pulls up the aerial*) Hallo? Base to Warden Nine.

There is a loud crackling noise. He recoils

Who is in charge of the bouncy castle?

Crackling noise

Bouncy castle!

More crackling

Well, find out and tell him to get over there damn quick.

More crackling noise

Because it's deflating, man! Deflate... Oh, dear God ... going down. Rapidly.

Ethel enters R, *dressed as Old Mother Hubbard. There are bones stitched to her dress. She carries a cardboard box and a carrier bag. She leans against the door exhausted*

Ethel It's pandemonium out there. There's no sign of the floats. Folks want to start buying. Someone's already got hit with a coconut. Mrs Godfrey's having one of her nosebleeds. St John's haven't come yet. The first aid tent's unmanned and... Oh! Are you on the phone? Sorry! Sorry! (*She tiptoes to the table and puts down the box and the bag. In a loud whisper*) Would you mind...

His ear to the phone, Geoffrey waves at her to wait. More crackling

Geoffrey Well, he'll have to blow it up *again*, won't he?
Ethel (*indicating the box*) Don't let no-one shift that box.

Geoffrey nods

I daren't put it down in the tea tent. I've already had a catering pack of margarine go missing. And in this carrier bag—here—bran tub prizes for Mavis. Oh, and wish her happy birthday.
Geoffrey (*into the phone*) No, I don't think it will make the slightest difference if the band plays in its shirtsleeves. It wouldn't make any difference if it played in its underpants. The resultant cacophony will be just as painful. (*He puts down the aerial and replaces the phone in his pocket*) Thump, thump, thump.
Ethel Oh, and Miss Pitt *is* here but she isn't wearing her costume.
Geoffrey (*gazing out of the window*) Right.
Ethel It's a shame, she'd have made a lovely Dick Whittington. They were very understanding at the hire shop. Gave her the deposit back.

Geoffrey (*still looking*) Good.

Ethel I must get on. I promised Mrs Martin a weak tea half an hour ago. She's in such a state. The man who paints seaviews on pebbles hasn't turned up and she doesn't know whether to leave him a space or count him absent.

Geoffrey Oh. (*He registers her words*) Pebbles?

Ethel Pebbles. People put them in the bottom of their fish tanks.

Geoffrey Why?

Ethel To give the fish somewhere to hide. (*She goes to the door*) You know, for all her lah de dah ways she's a hard worker. (*She speaks with false casualness*) We shall miss her when she goes. Funny, because I thought when they came here it was for good and all. Still, I suppose the army know what they're doing. (*She waits for him to comment*) Well, I must get on.

Ethel exits R

He takes his phone and speaks into it

Geoffrey Hallo? Hallo? Base to Warden Three. Hallo?

A crackling noise

Please go at once to the craft tent and tell Mrs Martin—Martin, man, Martin—that I would like to speak with her as soon as she is free.

More crackling

I. Me. The Vicar. As soon as possible.

He puts the phone away and, going to a chair, sits, his elbow on the table, his head resting in his hand

Mavis enters R. *She wears her mother's Edwardian wedding dress. It looks lovely from the front. Only when she turns is it apparent that it is far too small and undone all down the back*

Mavis I hope you're praying for rain, Vicar, then we can all go home and watch telly. (*She starts searching through bags*) What I'm looking for is more bits for me bran tub... Ethel did say she'd leave me some things. Has she been in?

Geoffrey looks at her

Ethel, Vicar. Has she been in?

Geoffrey What? Oh, yes.
Mavis Did she leave anything?
Geoffrey Leave anything? (*He looks at the table, sees the box*) Yes, that.

Mavis looks in the box he has indicated

Mavis Pink salmon? Kiddies don't want to dip in a bran tub and come up with
pink salmon. They wants plastic toys and liquorice sticks. She's getting
senile. Still, if that's what she's left that's what I'll take. (*She goes to pick
up the box*) It was me mother's.

Geoffrey looks at her noncomprehending

Me frock. Me mother's wedding dress. I know we're all supposed to be
fairy tale whatsits but what could I come as? (*With meaning*) At my age.
(*She waits in vain for him to wish her happy birthday*) Who are you, then?
Geoffrey What? Oh, Friar Tuck. And I feel ridiculous.
Mavis (*surveying him with a critical eye*) You don't look much different to
the way you look on Sundays. (*Picking up the box, she walks to the door*)
Geoffrey Mrs Partridge—did you know the Martins are leaving?
Mavis I have heard, yes.
Geoffrey My wife did say—and, of course, I've forgotten, where is it they're
going?
Mavis (*after some thought*) Now then ... somewhere foreign, was it?
Geoffrey Foreign?
Mavis I could be wrong. You know me, Vicar. Listens with me arse and
understands with me elbow. Another house on the market. None of 'em
lives here long enough to get buried.

She goes to the door R *as Marjorie enters, dressed as Hansel, hot and
perspiring*

Marjorie Christmas! It is hot and I mean hot. (*She flops into a chair*) Happy
birthday, Mavis.
Mavis (*with a look at Geoffrey*) Fancy you remembering! (*She turns to exit*)
Marjorie You're open all down the back.
Mavis Better than all down the front.

Mavis exits

Marjorie (*blowing down her shirt*) The WI float's stuck at the bottom of
Cherry Pie Hill. Not surprising with their combined weight giving us
Britain through the Ages. They're the first and nothing can get past. The
warden in charge of floats said can you let people know?

Geoffrey Know what?

Marjorie That none of the floats can move till the tractor gets there. So can you let people know. With your phone thingy.

Geoffrey Why didn't he ring me on *his* phone thingy?

Marjorie He tried. He's in a dip and couldn't get connected. (*She takes a hankie and dries inside her blouse*) Sod this for a game of soldiers. All morning grooming the ponies, walk 'em round, then find we can't get 'em through because twelve bloody lorries are blocking the road. Jack's holding them, they're kicking like stink, and we weren't speaking *before* we left home. Have you seen Angela?

Geoffrey Who?

Marjorie Angela. Angela Brownlee.

Geoffrey I don't think so... I may have. People are wearing such stupid clothes.

Marjorie (*looking at him*) Yes... So what are you going to do?

Geoffrey About what?

Marjorie The floats! The opening! Letting people know!

Geoffrey Nothing.

Marjorie Fine by me. Give him the message, I gave him the message... (*She stretches her legs out and hums tunelessly*)

He takes his phone

Geoffrey Hallo? Hallo? Base to any one who happens to be listening. (*He shakes the phone*) Hallo? Hallo? Is there anyone there?

Marjorie Two knocks for yes...

Geoffrey (*giving her one of his smiles*) I wonder if you could possibly——

Marjorie Troll from stall to stall, telling them there's a hitch with the floats? Nope. Sorry. One of the perks of being an atheist. You can say no to vicars.

Geoffrey Then would you mind—as an atheist—remaining here while I troll from stall to stall and inform my happy band that there's a "hitch" with the floats?

Marjorie Why do I have to stay here? There isn't anything worth pinching, is there?

Geoffrey (*going to the platform and lifting a curtain*) Three silver cups. A box of rosettes, and a birthday cake.

Marjorie Call in Securicor. Yes, I'll stay. Give me a chance to cool down.

Geoffrey Next to Christmas I hate this day more than any other.

Marjorie You know, you're better when you're on the toot.

He takes a flask from a pocket and drinks

Ah.

Geoffrey Are those ridiculous trousers made of leather?
Marjorie Yes. And I shall never again laugh at Morris Dancers.
Geoffrey Oh, I shall.

Geoffrey exits R

Marjorie leans back and closes her eyes

Ethel enters backwards, carrying a large tray of jam tarts. She is calling to Geoffrey

Ethel You'll have to get on and open it yourself then, Vicar! Floats or no floats! The crowd's turning very nasty. (*She turns and sees Marjorie*) Shouldn't you be on a horse?
Marjorie No, Ethel. I should be on a Caribbean island soaked in oil and drinking something long and cold…
Ethel Well, I've got the urn on… (*She puts the tray on the table*) I've had to bring these tarts inside. The flies are attacking and there are ants crawling up the table legs.
Marjorie I'm starving.
Ethel Twenty pence a tart.
Marjorie Keep 'em.

Ethel gives her one

Ta.
Ethel I don't envy Miss Brownlee on the kiddies' float. They'll be wanting a drink and wanting to wee. And a couple of 'em usually chuck up by the time they get here. Fumes from the diesel.
Marjorie (*shuddering*) Don't. Horse shit I can take…
Ethel Still, she'll handle it. Wonderful how she's come on, isn't it? Remember what a shy little thing she was when she first came?
Marjorie Oh yes…
Ethel And now—what's the word … liberated. She's liberated. Wouldn't you say?
Marjorie I wouldn't say anything, Ethel, but I gather other people would. And are.
Ethel Human nature, isn't it? Give 'em an inch and—where's my pink salmon?
Marjorie What?
Ethel Not five minutes ago I put that box on this table.

Marjorie makes a gesture of ignorance

Are you sure you didn't see the going of it?

Marjorie Oh, leave it out, Ethel...

Ethel Someone's walked out bold as brass with that salmon.

Gloria enters R, dressed in black

A box of pink salmon, Gloria. Twenty-four tins. Stolen from this table.

Gloria Oh, surely not?

Ethel starts to search for the box. She finds the carrier bag of rejects from the Good As New

Ethel And what are these doing here? They should be on the Good As New. (*She takes out Geoffrey's old trousers*) The things people chuck out. There's plenty of wear left in them. (*She holds them up*) They'd fit my Charlie for mucking about. Go through this lot, Gloria, while I look for that box. He's a seventeen collar.

Gloria looks through the clothes in an abstracted way. Ethel resumes the salmon hunt

Marjorie How are you doing then, Gloria?

Gloria Oh, I'm... I'm fine, thank you. Just seeing if I can be of use to anyone.

Marjorie You can be of use to me when the ponies eventually get here.

Ethel (*frantically searching for the salmon*) Of course she can't! Whatever would it look like? Her mother not cold and she's putting kiddies on horses.

Marjorie It would look like she's being very sensible and getting on with life. Oh, do keep still, Ethel!

Ethel It must be here... (*She finds the carrier bag with bran tub prizes*) Mavis is supposed to be fetching these.

Gloria I shouldn't really have come at all. I should be at home answering letters. There were so many...

Marjorie Can't you buy some of those card thingies?

Gloria Oh, Mother doesn't—didn't approve of notelets.

Ethel Drove me mad over that bran tub. Then don't pick up...

Sally enters R, dressed as the queen of hearts

Sally Why haven't we opened?

Marjorie The floats are held up.

Ethel Cherry Pie Hill. Like always.

Sally Where's Geoffrey?

Marjorie Trolling.

Sally looks at her

Telling people we can't open till the floats get here.
Sally Marvellous! I'm given a message that he wants to see me urgently…

Ethel is thrilled

…leave an idiot child holding the fort, dash over here and he's out there.
It's a shambles. A complete shambles. If the opening's seriously delayed
someone had better tell Councillor Williamson. He's already moaning that
he's got another fête to go to. Pompous little man. His dentures are
completely yellow, I can't bear to look at him. It's absolute hell out there.
Hilary Bagshott's sold half her plants already and people are kicking up
stink. Janet Goodlove refuses to price anything over fifty pence on the bric-
à-brac. Cynthia Brinscombe would go mad. I've put a twenty quid sticker
on my cherub.
Ethel Chipped cherub. (*She smiles brightly at Sally*)
Marjorie Calm down, Sal. By five o'clock we'll have made over two
thousand pounds and everyone will cheer and say what about next year.
Sally Next year, thank God, I shall be far, far away. Gloria, dear, how are we?
Gloria Oh, bearing up. Thank you.
Marjorie Scotland, isn't it?
Sally Hopefully. Depending on the survey. Of the house we want, not of
Scotland.
Marjorie By yon bonnie banks! Ah well, back to the fray. Oh! The hall
mustn't be left unattended. Apparently gangs of masked men are hiding in
the hedgerows waiting to swoop. (*Rising, she pulls the trousers away from
her bottom*) I'll never know why some people are kinky for leather…

Marjorie exits R

Ethel Very sudden, your move, Mrs Martin, isn't it?
Sally Oh no. It's been on the cards for months. Gloria, dear, you must come
round some evening, have a little sherry? Before we finally up sticks?
Gloria Oh, thank you…
Sally And needless to say, if you ever find yourself in Inverness?
Gloria That's very kind.
Sally If anyone does see Geoffrey, do tell him I answered his call.

Sally exits R

Ethel She's been doing that for months.
Gloria Ethel, Ethel, probably not a word of truth in it.

Ethel Truth enough for the Bishop to want to see him.

Gloria How do you know that?

Ethel Betty was dusting round when the call came. Bishops don't pick up a phone without reason. And I'll tell you something else—he didn't know she was going. Pretended he did, but he didn't. He went quite white.

Gloria (*looking out of the window*) The bouncy castle seems to have collapsed.

Ethel It will have. We was charged reduced rates. And I thought "Oh yes? And for why?"

The band starts to play

What's that from?

Gloria *Bless the Bride*. One of Mother's favourites. (*She holds her face and closes her eyes*)

Ethel Now you listen to me, Gloria. She was a good age and you were a wonderful daughter, you looked after her day and night, night and day. Without you, she'd have been gone long since. (*She holds a dress up to herself and then discards it*) When someone has a massive stroke and is just lying there, useless and senseless, well, just sometimes God knows what he's doing. Not often and not often enough, but when all's said and done, it was a blessing. It was, dear.

Gloria Yes. I think I'll just...

Gloria exits L

Mavis enters R

Ethel Why haven't you taken your bran tub prizes?

Mavis What?

Ethel narrows her eyes

I have taken them.

Ethel (*with the bag*) No, you haven't. They're here, look.

Mavis Shouldn't I have taken that salmon then?

Ethel Salmon? Pink salmon? Twenty-four tins?

Mavis When word got round I had a rush on.

Ethel Had a rush on? We haven't been opened yet!

Mavis Oh, I couldn't muck about waiting for no opening. I wants to get done and get gone.

Ethel Oh, Mavis! At this very moment I could throttle you. I could. I really could.

Mavis Don't go on at me. The vicar said to take them.
Ethel Did he! Well, he can pay for another twenty-four and they won't be
at cost.
Mavis What did I come in for?
Ethel How do I know?
Mavis I'll go back to where I was and see if it comes back to me. If I can
remember where I was.

Gloria enters L

I enjoyed the funeral. *Abide with Me*, you can't beat it. I thought to myself
sitting there, I thought, I expect I'll be the next to go.

Ethel gives her a look that says she wouldn't mind if she was

And I hope you're not blaming yourself.
Gloria Blaming myself?
Ethel Don't talk daft. What's she got to blame herself for?
Mavis Thinking there was more she could have done. (*To Gloria*) She was
nearly ninety, couldn't move, and was a burden to you and herself. If she'd
been a spaniel you'd have had her put down.

Mavis exits R

Ethel 'Cept you wouldn't have, would you?
Gloria Probably not.
Ethel (*musing*) Shall I pop back home and boil some eggs … or shall I grate
another pound of strong cheddar…
Gloria I've a larder full of tinned pilchards. Mother loves—loved them.
Ethel No, ta, Gloria, thanks all the same. People don't like the black bits. But
if push comes to shove…

Pauline enters R. *She puts a large box on the table*

Mind my tarts!
Pauline I'm afraid Janet Goodlove's had a disaster. (*She takes out the top
half of the cherub*)
Ethel Where's the rest of it?
Pauline In here. In bits.
Ethel Coconut shy?
Pauline Welly boot throwing. One of the Treadwells broke all previous
records.
Ethel They've no right throwing before we've opened.

Pauline Would you like to tell them? Gloria, how are you? So brave of you to come.

Gloria Oh, I'm fine. Just … you know.

Pauline She was a great age…

Gloria So people keep saying.

Sally enters R. *She sees the cherub*

Sally Is that my cherub?

Pauline What's left of it. An accident, I'm afraid.

Sally Aren't people—savages. I could weep.

Ethel Have you caught up with the vicar? He's not been back in.

Sally What? Oh, no. (*She strokes the cherub*) I shouldn't have let you go…

Pauline (*with cold courtesy*) Can I help? If you have a message for—my husband?

Sally Actually he wanted to see me.

Pauline Ah. Then of course he must see *you,* mustn't he?

Pauline exits R

Sally starts looking for something

Ethel Have you lost something, Mrs Martin?

Sally It's my pebble man. He's arrived, but—wouldn't you know—he's forgotten his sea green cloth. He spreads it over the table to set of his wares. I wondered if…

Gloria There's a large tablecloth in the kitchen. Or there was. I'll have a look. It's multi-floral, I'm afraid.

Gloria exits L

Sally I hardly think multi-floral will do much for his sea views. However, if the silly man arrives without——

Ethel Mrs Morris seemed a bit off, didn't she?

Sally Did she?

Ethel Mm. Mind you, she's not been herself all this year. People have remarked on it. I suppose she's under a lot of strain. One way and another. Church affairs … village affairs … any other affairs … it all falls on her, doesn't it?

Sally (*with a cloth*) This might do…

Ethel And it's not cos he's drinking. He's not been seen in the *Coach and Horses* for … oh, months.

Sally (*putting it down*) No, I think not…

Ethel Folks have been wondering if he's taken up something else? Some new hobby, perhaps? What do you think?

Sally I wouldn't know.

Ethel Oh? I thought you ... socialised together.

Gloria enters with a large flowered tablecloth

Gloria Here we are. The odd tea stain, but a little judicious placing of pebbles should cover the worst.

Sally Thank you. (*She takes the cloth*) Oh, while I think of it, Mrs Swift, I mentioned that we're having a small gathering to say farewell to all our friends.

Ethel And you was wanting cold meats and cheeses, yes, I've had a word with— —

Sally Do you know—on reflection I think I'll use caterers. So much less strain.

Ethel (*tight-lipped*) Right, then. I'll cancel the order to my wholesalers.

Sally Thank you.

Sally exits

Ethel Bitch. That was deliberate nastiness.

Gloria Yes, I rather think it was... What did you say to her?

Ethel looks at her with an innocent expression

Angela enters R, *dressed as Snow White*

Angela Ta-ra! We won the prize!

Ethel What prize?

Angela For the best float!

Ethel Are you telling me the floats are here?

Angela Hours ago! The WI got down and pushed.

Ethel My tea tent will be packed out. Whenever you feel like it, Gloria, I'll be glad of a washer upper.

Ethel exits

Angela I've come in here for a quick fag. Can't let the kids see Miss having a puff. (*She takes out a packet of cigarettes. Offers them to Gloria*)

Gloria No, thank you. Er ... really and truly, this is a non-smoking area.

Angela I won't tell, if you don't. (*She lights a cigarette*) Oh, sorry to hear about your mother.

Gloria Thank you.

Angela Ninety-three, was it?

Gloria No, no, she'll be—would have been—eighty-eight in September. There is a clause in the insurance, you know. About smoking.

Angela Just a couple more puffs. (*She inhales on the cigarette*) Could you still go to Africa?

Gloria Sorry?

Angela Africa, don't you remember? You said there was a job in Africa, nursing, was it? And your mother wouldn't let you go.

Gloria Oh! Africa ... yes.

Angela I thought that was really sad when you told me.

Gloria I wonder if you could wait here till someone comes? The hall mustn't be left unattended.

Angela Yup. I'll hold the fort!

Gloria Please do put that cigarette out. (*She pauses*) Africa! I get prickly heat if I sit by a light bulb.

Gloria exits R

Angela has one last puff, then stubs her cigarette out. She sees the binoculars. Taking them to the window, she looks out, then reverses them and looks through the opposite end

Marjorie enters R. *She sees Angela, watches her for a moment*

Marjorie Well, well. If it isn't Cinderella. (*She looks around*) No sign of Buttons...

Angela (*without turning*) Snow White actually.

Marjorie Whatever. It's ... very pretty.

Angela Everyone's tiny...

Marjorie Can you see the oik? Is he tiny?

Angela doesn't respond

You do know there's a lot of talk.

Angela Surprise, surprise.

Marjorie I just don't want you to be ... hurt.

Angela Yes, you do. You want me to be desperately hurt.

Marjorie I don't, Angel! God, I don't. You know how I feel about you.

Angela sighs

Angel, please. I ring you—you put the phone down. I try to talk to you, you walk away, I must have written a hundred letters——

Angela Please, Marjorie…
Marjorie I couldn't sleep last night, knowing I'd see you today.
Angela Stop it.
Marjorie It's over with me and Jack. Finished. She's moving out.
Angela I'm sorry. I really am. But it's got nothing to do with me. (*She moves towards the door*)
Marjorie Don't go, please, can't we just talk?
Angela There is nothing to talk about.
Marjorie There's everything to talk about——
Angela This is so … ridiculous.
Marjorie Ridiculous? And everything that happened between us? Was that ridiculous? When you said I was the best, the most wonderful, the most caring——
Angela I was … experimenting.
Marjorie Really? Then you were a bloody quick learner. Every second we could be together. Phone calls, meetings, letters——
Angela I want them back.

Marjorie looks at her

The letters. I … want them back.
Marjorie Want them back? Why do you… Oh. I see. (*She moves close, speaks in a hoarse whisper*) What's it worth? Fifty quid a letter? Of course you can have them back.
Angela Thank you.
Marjorie What I can't stand is that you hate me. Why do you? Why?
Angela I don't hate you. I hate what happened. It makes me sick when I think of it.
Marjorie What happened was we loved each other. Didn't we?
Angela Please…
Marjorie I'll do anything you want, Angel. Anything. We can leave here, go away, start somewhere new——
Angela Start what? (*Very deliberately*) It is over.
Marjorie Then tell me why "it is over"? One letter, two months ago, saying you wouldn't be seeing me again. And no reason. It's not fair——
Angela Raymond said…
Marjorie Sorry? Sorry? Raymond said? You've talked about us—to him?
Angela I had to. He'd heard rumours—I said you had a thing about me and…
Marjorie And what? Forced you into bed—ripped your clothes off—gave you your first proper orgasm—that sort of a thing?
Angela I was young, stupid, new to the village. And you just … swooped in on me.
Marjorie Oh, please!

Angela And I didn't know any better.

Marjorie I don't believe this. Young and new to the village, yes. But stupid? No, never that. Well, not till you started bonking the oik.

Angela It's a normal healthy relationship. And that's what you hate.

Marjorie Normal healthy—he's an eighteen year-old tearaway, who's screwed every girl in the village, will never hold down a job in his life, and you trail round after him like a bitch on heat. No, that's insulting to bitches. With their delicate sense of smell they'd walk on by.

Angela Normal healthy male female relationship. He was nineteen last week. And he hasn't screwed every girl in the village.

Marjorie Every other then. It's just sex, isn't it? It can't be anything else.

Angela We do lots of things together.

Marjorie I bet. Got a big one, has he?

Angela Yes. Very. And it doesn't run on batteries.

Marjorie slaps her face

That was a silly thing to do.

Marjorie I'm sorry, I'm so sorry, but…

Angela It might have hurt the baby.

Marjorie What?

Angela Baby. His and mine.

Marjorie looks at her, stunned

But please don't start knitting. I'm probably going to have an abortion.

Marjorie Angel, no. Don't. Keep it. Have it. We'll be all right. I'll look after you. It can be ours, our baby. I'll never mention him or say anything. Please, oh, I beg you, don't, don't kill it?

Angela It has nothing—nothing—nothing to do with you.

Marjorie But—Angel…

Mavis enters R

Mavis There's a queue to that toilet tent like you wouldn't believe. (*She sees Angela*) You're a stranger. I've missed you popping in.

Angela Sorry. I'll … try and come round soon.

Angela exits R

Marjorie looks after her, then sits, in total misery

Mavis She's not a bad lass. Bit stupid, but age'll cure that. Had words, have you?

Marjorie nods

Ah well, I don't expect she——
Marjorie She's pregnant.
Mavis She will be. They always hit the bull's-eye, them Treadwells.

Marjorie starts to cry. Mavis goes to her

Come on, my duck, let it out. (*She puts her arms round a sobbing Marjorie*) If it ain't one thing, it's another... (*She rocks Marjorie back and forth and croons a lullaby*)

SCENE 2

The village hall. Four hours later. Total chaos

Geoffrey sits behind the table wearily counting the takings

Geoffrey One, two, three, four——

Ethel enters R *with a tray of sandwiches*

—five, six, seven, eight——

Ethel puts the tray on the table

—nine, ten, eleven, twelve——

Mavis enters with a tray of sausage rolls

—thirteen, fourteen, fifteen, sixteen——

Ethel indicates to put the tray on the table

—seventeen, eighteen, nineteen, twenty——

Ethel beckons Mavis to follow her to the door R

Mavis (*in a loud whisper*) What's happening to them sausage rolls?
Ethel (*in a loud whisper*) Us'll have them later with a cup of tea.
Mavis What?
Geoffrey (*loudly*) Us'll have them later with a cup of tea.

Mavis Oh, I'll be gone by then.
Ethel So you keep saying. But you're still here.

Mavis and Ethel exit

Geoffrey Twenty, twenty-one— (*he thinks*) twenty-three— (*he thinks*)
twenty-one... Oh ... sod. (*In frustration, he pushes the money away, gets
up and stretches*)

Pauline enters R with a large box

Pauline I thought Miss Pitt was helping you?
Geoffrey So did I.
Pauline I'll send her in. (*She puts the box on the floor, stands and stretches.
She puts her hands in the small of her back, makes a face of pain*)

Geoffrey looks at her

Geoffrey Would you like me to ... rub your back?
Pauline No. I'd like you to give me a swig from the flask you're hiding in
your pocket.

He gives it to her. She drinks and hands it back

Geoffrey You look tired.
Pauline Tired? (*She laughs*) Yes, I'm tired.
Geoffrey You work very hard at these ... events.
Pauline Yes. I might go away for a while.
Geoffrey This is rather ... sudden, isn't it?
Pauline Not really.
Geoffrey And will you—are you—coming back?
Pauline Probably. Possibly. I ... don't know.
Geoffrey I see. I would understand. If you—didn't.

She laughs

What? What is it?
Pauline Friar Tuck and Maid Marian are discussing their marriage. I find that
amusing. Don't you?
Geoffrey Pauline, I do know that our—your life has been...
Pauline Sheer bloody hell, actually.
Geoffrey Perhaps tonight we could——
Pauline I haven't had a life, Geoffrey. I've had an existence. A miserable

soul-destroying hollow empty existence. For years and years and years. Walking around with an air of saintliness that's made *me* feel sick, so God knows what it's done to other people. Every time I leave a room with you— "Why does she stay? How does she put up with him? Did you see him last Tuesday?" And always right up to the wire then the famous charm and the smile of great sincerity and you just manage to hang on in there. Blast you.

Geoffrey Why did you stay?

Pauline You ask me that? You'd better brush up your book of common prayer. Till death us do part, isn't it? And—because I loved you. Loved. Past tense. I don't any more. Not for a long time. Long before you started all this nonsense with her.

Geoffrey That's … over.

Pauline Really? I don't give a damn. In fact maybe I'm sorry. You were marginally pleasanter for a while. I wonder who told the Bishop.

Geoffrey One of my flock, I suppose.

Pauline Will he chuck you out?

Geoffrey Not if I humbly apologise and promise to keep my cassock clean in future. And…

Pauline And if I tell him how much strain you've been under and that I intend to support you fully.

Geoffrey And will you? Tell him that?

Pauline Good heavens! A decision. I haven't made one of those for years. I don't know. I really don't know.

Sally enters R. *She holds an unbroken rifle*

Pauline gasps

Sally Major Godfrey's poodle has bitten Janet Goodlove. And her husband got his rifle to shoot it. I persuaded him to hand it over. But I haven't the faintest idea what to——

Geoffrey carefully takes the rifle and breaks it. Sally sighs with relief

Thank you.

Geoffrey I'll put it in the kitchen.

Pauline High up!

Geoffrey Bloody high up!

Geoffrey exits L

Sally Feelings are running a little high out there. I think someone needs to defuse the situation.

Pauline Someone kind and saintly. (*She goes to the door* R) Serious bite?
Sally No, just a nibble really. But she's very upset.
Pauline Of course she is. It's an ill-tempered little bitch. And a nibble can hurt just as much as a bite.

Pauline exits R

Geoffrey enters from the kitchen

Geoffrey I hear you're moving?
Sally Yes.
Geoffrey You didn't think it necessary to mention it? I didn't enjoy being told by Mrs Swift.
Sally I didn't really think it concerned you. After all we haven't seen each other since you ended our little ... skirmish.
Geoffrey Skirmish? We committed adultery.
Sally How biblical.
Geoffrey I still think you might have——
Sally Geoffrey, we had an affair, we were lovers for five months. Then a sudden phone call. "I can't see you any more. Don't ask me why." So I have neither asked you—nor told you—anything.
Geoffrey I ended it because you wanted me to love you——

She starts to speak

Yes, you did. I know you did. And I couldn't. Because there is no love in me. But I've missed you, oh, I've missed you. So many times I've wanted to——
Sally There is something I should have told you. Someone wrote Colin a letter.
Geoffrey About us?
Sally Of course about us! What did you think? The water rates?

Ethel enters R. *She senses the atmosphere and is thrilled*

Ethel Sorry to interrupt—the craft tent's coming down, Mrs Martin.
Sally Oh, right.
Ethel Just so's you know.
Sally Thank you.
Ethel And the bouncy castle won't deflate. Two hours to get it up and now it won't come down.

They do not respond

I'll go then.

Ethel exits R

Geoffrey Was it her?
Sally Who wrote the letter? Possibly. What does it matter? Anyway, he hit
me and the roof and asked for a posting.
Geoffrey Why didn't he … come and see me?
Sally What for? Spiritual guidance? He hates scenes. Anyway, he's been
playing away for years.

He looks at her

Committing adultery!
Geoffrey But—if he's been unfaithful then why is he——
Sally Because he does it all the time. He always has. It's a first for me, so he's
worried.
Geoffrey Why didn't you tell me before? About the letter?
Sally I hate scenes too. And you might have said something stupid like "Let's
run away together".
Geoffrey I still might.
Sally Oh please! Major's wife runs off with Vicar. Vicar runs off with
Major's wife. It would totally wreck his career.
Geoffrey (*quietly*) And mine.
Sally God, socially one would be ruined. And yes, I know how selfish that
sounds, but it matters to me. The entertaining, the mess functions, the
position. It … matters. It's been my life. I've had nothing else.
Geoffrey I know. And I'm sorry. Very sorry.

Sally goes to the door R

Sally Look, he probably won't, but he did say something about speaking to
a "Higher Authority" and I don't think he meant God.
Geoffrey No. He meant the Bishop. And he obviously has.
Sally Oh. (*She sighs*) Sorry. Still, you can always lie. I'll back you if needs be.
Geoffrey I wouldn't lie.
Sally No, you wouldn't, would you? (*She goes back and kisses his cheek*)
Take care.

Sally exits R

*He takes the flask out. He tries to drink but it's empty. He goes to the table.
He sits and starts to count the money*

Marjorie enters R

She takes a sausage roll, eats it, and watches him

Marjorie Warden number three—I've no idea what his name is—says can
you suggest what they can do to get the bouncy castle down?
Geoffrey Stick a pin in it.
Marjorie It's pin proof.
Geoffrey Cut it loose and let it float away.
Marjorie It's a serious question.
Geoffrey It's a serious answer.

She looks at him then sits. She makes little piles of the coins

Marjorie What you said earlier, about hating today and hating Christmas
Day and——
Geoffrey I had actually counted those.
Marjorie Oh, sorry. But I was thinking—why do you stick at all this? All
this vicar stuff. Because you obviously hate it.
Geoffrey Do I?
Marjorie Oh, come on! You're more of an atheist that I am. Why did you
give up advertising and start all this lark?
Geoffrey I had a vocation.

She looks at him in disbelief

You seem surprised.
Marjorie I was wondering what happened to it?
Geoffrey A question I ask myself daily. (*He thinks for a while*) When I was
young, I had acne. I don't know what they call it now, testosterone
probably—but in my youth it was acne. And everyone said "You'll wake
up one day and it will be gone". I didn't believe them. I thought I'd go
through life with a face like the craters of the moon. But do you know they
were right. One morning I woke up, looked in the mirror and—gone. I
hadn't seen it going. But it was gone. And never returned. (*He looks at her*)
Time passes, as they say in all good fairy tales. Twenty years in fact. During
which time I convince my dear wife and myself that I am meant to be a
priest and give to God all I have to give. And I woke up one morning, knelt
to say my morning prayers and—gone. Overnight. My faith. My belief.
The purpose of my existence. Gone. Like my acne. Gone. And for no
reason. I hadn't buried a child or watched a young person die a painful
lingering death or struggled to believe. I went to bed with a faith and woke
up with none.

Marjorie Did you… (*she shrugs*) look for it?

Geoffrey Oh yes. I had the house to pieces. Has anyone seen my faith, I asked? I had it yesterday and now I can't find it anywhere.

Marjorie But—how can you hand out all that love thy neighbour crap when you don't believe it?

Geoffrey Oh, but I do. That's the living hell of it. I do believe, I just can't find it. I just can't find it. With booze or without. Nor it would seem a satisfactory substitute.

Marjorie You and old frilly knickers? People aren't talking about that any more. They're talking about Angela.

Geoffrey Who?

Marjorie laughs

Marjorie Never mind. (*She watches him count the money*) So what are you waiting for? Your pension?

Geoffrey No, my absolution.

Marjorie You poor old bugger. (*She puts a hand over his*)

Ethel and Mavis enter R. *Ethel sees the hand*

Ethel Is it all right to come in?

Marjorie Do. We're practising charismatic Christianity. Aren't we, Vicar?

Geoffrey In its most primitive form.

Ethel Oh. Are we going to start doing it on Sundays? People won't like it.

Geoffrey I don't suppose they will. I don't suppose they will… (*He stands and gently touches Marjorie's hair*)

Geoffrey exits L

Ethel He wasn't—you know—was he?

Marjorie No, Ethel. He wasn't you know. And he wouldn't have got far with me if he had you know. Because as you very well know, I'm not that kind of a girl.

Marjorie exits R

Ethel There's things going on in this parish, Mavis, that'd make a saint turn up his toes.

Mavis It was worse in my day. Let's get stuck into them sausage rolls.

Ethel Later, Mavis. We've to take them boxes out so's they can start going to the tip. Hold your arms out.

Mavis Don't overload me.

Ethel Stop moaning, Mavis.

Ethel puts boxes on Mavis' outstretched arms

Gloria enters R

Gloria I've been sent to help Vicar with the counting.
Ethel He's in the kitchen. Pile me up with them boxes. (*She stretches her arms out*)

Gloria puts boxes on Ethel's arms

Ta, that'll do. They're going to the tip.

Gloria opens the door R

Ethel and Mavis exit

There is the sound of boxes falling

(*Off*) Oh Mavis!

Gloria shuts the door. She goes to the table, starts to make sense of the money

Geoffrey enters. He has a glass of water

She smiles at him

Gloria I'll finish off, shall I ?
Geoffrey Please....(*He sits next to her*)
Gloria Such a hot day.You must be longing to go home and .. .
Geoffrey Take my frock off. Yes. (*He drinks the last of the water*) Water, I promise you.

She opens her bag and hands him a small bottle of brandy

Gloria I kept it for Mother.

He takes it. Pours some into his glass. Hands it back

No, keep it.
Geoffrey Thank you. (*He drinks*) Thank you very much.

She smiles at him. He watches her count the money

Do you know, Miss Pitt, you are probably the only truly good person I have ever met.

She looks at him, then starts to cry. He is disconcerted and doesn't know what to do. Eventually he pats her shoulder

Gloria I'm so sorry...

Geoffrey My dear, you shouldn't have come. So soon after losing your mother. You shouldn't have come. I know—we all know—how much you must miss her. (*He starts to rise*) Let me find someone to take you home.

Gloria No, please, no.

Geoffrey But——

Gloria Not yet. I must talk to you. And you must tell me what to do. Please?

Geoffrey What to do? Well, perhaps, after some time has passed, you may consider ... moving? Mm? Fresh start? New surroundings? Not immediately, of course, but perhaps in a while——

Gloria I killed her.

He looks at her

I did. I killed her. And I don't know what to do. (*She looks at him in utter misery*)

He offers her the brandy bottle. She shakes her head. Then she rises and goes to the window. She speaks to him while looking out

She was always so capable, so competent. And I was always so stupid. Or felt stupid. From when I was a child. "Give it to me, give it to me," she used to say. "You'll break it, you'll drop it, you'll burn it." So I did. Bottles to be opened. Buttons to be sewn on. Scones to be made. I gave them all to her because she was so much better at it than me. Better at everything. And then when I wanted to leave home—"You? Live alone? How ever would you manage?" So I stayed. Because I believed her, you see. And I was ... frightened. So I stayed. Lived my whole life here. With her. But as she grew old and infirm and needed me more and more and I had to do everything, I realized I wasn't stupid. No, I could do anything. But it was too late. I'd believed her for too long. She cheated me. To keep me. And I hated her.

Geoffrey Did you ... tell her that?

Gloria No. How could I? I even, at appropriate moments, told her I loved her.

Geoffrey What do you mean? Appropriate moments?

Gloria When she cried, and said she was a burden to me, and when she was in pain. It was all I could think of to comfort her.

Geoffrey So … even though you hated her you thought of ways to comfort her.

Gloria What else could I do?

Geoffrey There are places where——

Gloria A Home, you mean? No, I couldn't have done that. Oh, I know there are some good ones where they would probably have been kind, but they wouldn't have known what she liked. Her little ways. How to deal with her. She would have been wretched.

Geoffrey Yet … you hated her.

Gloria Yes.

Geoffrey I think not.

Gloria But I killed her.

Geoffrey Oh yes, so you did.

Gloria She just lay there, you know. Day after day she just … just lay there. Demanding nothing any more.

Geoffrey Except your constant care and attention.

Gloria Which I could have given her. I was giving her until… I was sorting through her things. I knew it would have to be done eventually and I thought it would be less painful if I did it while—while she was alive. And in a drawer of her bureau I found a bundle of letters. (*She looks out of the window*) The bouncy castle is still inflated.

Geoffrey I know. Letters, you say?

Gloria Yes. When I was fifty—and Mother could still manage—I went on holiday, just for a week, to Scarborough. So bracing. And I met a man. He was my age, a widower, we shared a table at the guest house. It was very … pleasant. We spent every day together. Chatting, walking, talking, listening to the band. I told him about Mother, he told me about his married daughter, it was … so good. So … companionable. At the end of the week we exchanged addresses. He kissed me goodbye. Kissed me. Held me in his arms and kissed me. And … when I came home I waited for him to write. He said he would. And I waited. And I waited. But nothing. So I assumed that he had decided not to keep in touch. I told Mother about him, of course. She was … surprisingly good about it. Said I must ask him to stay. But he didn't write.

Geoffrey Why didn't you write to him?

Gloria I was going to. But Mother said that would be pushing myself on him. So—I didn't.

Geoffrey And you found letters from him. That your mother had kept.

Gloria Read and kept. Eight letters. The first asking me to go and stay because he missed me very much and was hoping our friendship could continue. The second asking why I hadn't replied because he was missing me more each day. Then five more at weekly intervals. Then the last one, very hurt and very sad. Saying goodbye. I took them to the bed. And I read them to her. She was unconscious, of course, but they say hearing is the last sense to go so I read them to her. I could have married him, I told her. I could have been loved. Then I took a pillow and held it over her face. Then I called Dr O'Connor. Who pronounced her dead and gave me something for the shock. Which I needed. I'd better go to the police, hadn't I?

Geoffrey Not just yet. Come and sit down.

She returns and sits

Loved her, hated her, what does it matter? You were there. Duty was done. And seemingly done with affection. And occasional words of love even if untrue. Which I doubt.

She goes to speak. He puts a finger to her lips

To do one's duty, when every fibre, every nerve end is screaming no, no, no. That is a love greater than any other. Did she love you? Yes, probably, as the parasite loves the dog it lives off. Did she wrong you? Most certainly and most dreadfully. Did you do wrong? Yes, but most understandably. And if you go to the police—then what? Months of waiting, a painful public disclosure of your private life, sensation for the masses on page five of the *Telegraph*. And then a suspended sentence which you have already given yourself. My dear, don't waste the rest of your time on this miserable planet. Mourn, grieve, whip yourself if you must. Then move on. And forgive yourself, I beg you. Because you are most truly sorry. Which cannot be said of many of us sinners.

Gloria Am I? Truly sorry?

Geoffrey Why else would you have told me?

Gloria God will never forgive me.

Geoffrey I rather think he has to. But—for the little it's worth, you have my forgiveness and … my blessing.

Gloria Thank you. Thank you. You're the only person I could have told.

Geoffrey Really? That's … very kind. (*Unable to show emotion in front of her, he picks up his glass*) Excuse me.

Geoffrey exits L

Gloria sits for a moment, then begins to count the money in a business-like manner

Ethel and Mavis enter R. *Ethel is beside herself with excitement*

Ethel There's a fight going on. Real scrap, isn't it, Mavis?

Mavis I'm surprised we've got this far without.
Ethel I said there's a fight going on, Gloria!
Gloria Yes. I heard.

Pauline enters R

Ethel What's happening?
Pauline The police are on their way.
Ethel Should I get the vicar?
Gloria He's in the kitchen.
Pauline Why? What possible use could he be?

Gloria looks at her

Mavis Them Treadwells, always trouble. The grandfather was the worst.
One time he wrecked the beer tent and put ten men in hospital. All because
he didn't win with his onions.
Ethel I'm going back out.
Mavis Mind yourself. They've no respect for wimmin.
Ethel I'm going to watch 'em, Mavis. Not separate 'em.

Ethel exits R

Gloria What's the trouble this time?
Pauline Oh, Raymond Treadwell was ... talking to someone else's
girlfriend and — —
Mavis He had his hand up her skirt!
Pauline Whatever—the young man took exception and all hell broke loose.
The police can sort it out. (*She looks at her watch*) Now, what about getting
the rest of these boxes outside?

Marjorie and Sally enter R

Marjorie Have you seen what's going on out there? It's like the barn raising
in *Seven Brides for Seven Brothers*.
Pauline The police are on the way.
Sally They're here, actually. Joining in with gusto. Any excuse to wield a
baton.

Mavis goes to the window

Mavis Oh, drat.
Pauline What?

Mavis It's all over. They're shoving 'em in the vans. Hang on—Iris Treadwell's just knocked a copper's hat off. Now they're shoving her in as well. (*She remains looking out of the window*)

Ethel rushes in R and goes to Marjorie

Ethel You're wanted. Urgent.
Marjorie Me? I'm not part of the riot squad.
Ethel (*in a falsely lowered voice*) It's Miss Brownlee. She got mixed up in the fighting and she's collapsed.
Marjorie What?
Ethel Doubled up she is. In agonies. Asking for you.
Marjorie Me?
Ethel "Get Mugsy" she screamed. "Get Mugsy." If I didn't know better I'd say she was... (*She mouths the word*) Miscarrying.
Marjorie What?
Mavis Miscarrying. She is. I can see from here.

Marjorie exits R

Ethel Fancy, the first time in all these years we've had to call an ambulance! I wish I'd brought me camera!

Ethel exits R

Pauline I'd better go. (*She sighs*) Another infant teacher bites the dust. And we can't blame the National Curriculum.

Pauline exits R

Sally Scotland is going to seem awfully dull after this...
Gloria (*writing*) One thousand and ninety-eight pounds so far ... excellent. (*She rises*) The Vicar's in the kitchen. Will you tell him I've finished?
Mavis I will, my duck. And Gloria—get out of that black. It drains you something awful.

Gloria exits R

Sally Well. After all the excitement I really think I'm going to go home, have a long hot bath, pour me a stiff G and T, and put witch hazel pads on my eyes. So dusty out there... (*She turns for the door*)
Mavis You're a very wicked woman.
Sally I beg your pardon?

Mavis You heard. She won't say nothing on account of being a lady, but I'm going to tell you. What you've done here these past months was wicked. Sinful. And shameless.

Sally You wrote to my husband, didn't you?

Mavis No. Cos I wouldn't have hurt him. (*She nods towards the door* L) Not like you have.

Sally I don't have to listen to this——

Mavis He was struggling when you arrived. But managing. Just. Hanging on and she was hanging on with him. Now, Lord knows what he'll do. Cos he's finished here. Can't hold his head up. (*She looks out of the window*)

There is the sound of a rifle shot. Sally screams

(*Without turning*) That'll be him, poor soul. Ending it. For the best, really.

Sally stands. Terrified. She moves towards the kitchen, then sobs and exits R

After a moment Geoffrey enters L

Nice one, Vicar, I saw you poke that rifle out the window and I thought "He's going for that bouncy castle", I thought.

Geoffrey Seemed the most expedient way of getting it down. And very satisfying.

Mavis You can do it to me when my time's up. I don't never want to be a burden. (*She goes to the curtain and takes out her cake*) What a surprise!

Geoffrey If I had a match I'd——

Mavis takes a box of matches from her pocket and lights one candle, then takes a gift-wrapped parcel from behind the curtain

Mavis Tell 'em I took me chocolates. Ta ta. (*She moves to the door*)

Geoffrey Mrs Partridge…

She stops and looks at him

…it's a little late but—happy birthday.

Mavis smiles at him and exits R

Geoffrey looks at the cake, then at the candle. He puts his fingers together. He closes his eyes, wishing or maybe praying

Pauline enters R *and is visibly relieved to see him*

He opens his eyes, blows the candle out. He looks at Pauline and gives her a smile of great charm and seemingly utter sincerity. He holds out a hand. She stands motionless, looking at him. After a moment——

——the CURTAINS *fall*

FURNITURE AND PROPERTY LIST

Further dressing may be added at the director's discretion

ACT I

SCENE 1

On stage: Drooping curtains at rear as if concealing a platform
Drooping floral curtains on window
Cumbersome radiator. *Under it*: rubbish
Notice board with many pieces of paper tacked up
Folded trestle tables
Stack of chairs
Remnants of Christmas: drooping paper chain, tinsel, sprig of dead
holly

Off stage: Sit-up and beg bicycle. *In its basket*: ancient and bulging briefcase
containing files, agendas, papers, pencils (**Gloria**)
Capacious bag. *In it*: 2 packets of biscuits (**Pauline**)
Large bag containing knitting of large colourful blanket and crotchet
hook (**Mavis**)
Tea things (**Angela**)
Handbag, stone cherub wrapped in blanket (**Sally**)

Personal: **Gloria:** glasses, newspaper

SCENE 2

Set: Teacups
Agendas
Pile of notes
Mavis's knitting (now longer)
Pauline's gavel
Compact and make-up in **Sally**'s bag

Off stage: Cup of tea (**Angela**)

ACT II

Scene 1

On stage: As for Act I with the exception of the Christmas decorations and the
    addition of:
    Erected trestle table
    Cardboard boxes
    Plastic bags. *On one of them*: binoculars
    Chairs
    On platform behind curtain: 3 silver cups, box of rosettes, birthday
    cake with candles, gift-wrapped parcel
    Cloth

Off stage: Bulging carrier bags containing old clothes (**Pauline**)
    Cardboard box, carrier bag with bran tub prizes (**Ethel**)
    Large tray of jam tarts (**Ethel**)
    Large box containing top half of cherub (**Pauline**)
    Large flowered tablecloth (**Gloria**)

Personal: **Geoffrey:** mobile phone, flask
    Marjorie: handkerchief
    Angela: packet of cigarettes, lighter

Scene 2

Set: Money

Off stage: Tray of sandwiches (**Ethel**)
    Tray of sausage rolls (**Mavis**)
    Large box (**Pauline**)
    Rifle (**Sally**)
    Glass of water (**Geoffrey**)
    Bag containing small bottle of brandy (**Gloria**)
    Large cardboard box containing broken cherub (**Pauline**)

Personal: **Geoffrey:** flask
    Gloria: pen
    Pauline: watch
    Mavis: box of matches

LIGHTING PLOT

Property fittings required: nil
1 interior setting. The same throughout

ACT I

To open: Dim house lights

ACT I, Scene 1

To open: Evening lighting

Cue 1   **Ethel** switches on a light   (Page 2)
               Bring up general lighting

ACT I, Scene 2

To open: Overall general lighting

No cues

ACT II, Scene 1

To open: Overall summertime lighting

No cues

ACT II, Scene 2

To open: Overall afternoon lighting

No cues

EFFECTS PLOT

ACT I

Cue 1   **Ethel** puts a finger in her mouth   (Page 2)
           Sound of motor bike revving outside

Cue 2   **Ethel** looks towards door   (Page 2)
           Sound of bike pulling away

ACT II

Cue 3   To open Scene 1   (Page 29)
           Banging and shouting off

Cue 4   **Geoffrey**: "Base to Warden Nine."   (Page 30)
           Loud crackling noise

Cue 5   **Geoffrey**: "Who is in charge of the bouncy castle?"   (Page 30)
           Crackling noise

Cue 6   **Geoffrey**: "Bouncy castle!"   (Page 31)
           More crackling noise

Cue 7   **Geoffrey**: "...to get over there damn quick."   (Page 31)
           More crackling noise

Cue 8   **Geoffrey** waves at **Ethel** to wait   (Page 31)
           More crackling noise

Cue 9   **Geoffrey**: "Base to Warden Three. Hallo?"   (Page 32)
           Crackling noise

Cue 10   **Geoffrey**: "...speak with her as soon as she is free." (Page 32)
           More crackling noise

Cue 11   **Ethel**: "Oh yes? And for why?"   (Page 38)
           Start band playing

Cue 12   **Mavis** looks out of the window   (Page 58)
               Sound of rifle shot